BENNY ANDERSEN

SELECTED POEMS

D1603152

THE LOCKERT LIBRARY OF
POETRY IN TRANSLATION
FOR OTHER TITLES IN
THE LOCKERT LIBRARY
SEE PAGE 74

Benny Andersen
Selected Poems

TRANSLATED BY

ALEXANDER TAYLOR

PRINCETON UNIVERSITY

PRESS

distributed by Curbstone Press
Copyright © 1975 Princeton University Press
All Rights Reserved

ISBN: 1-880684-53-5   n)

LCC: 74-27874 (Bilingual clothbound edition)
LCC: 74-27873 (English paperback edition)

The poems in Danish, in the bilingual clothbound
edition, were first published by Borgens Forlag A/S,
Copenhagen, Denmark, in the following volumes:
Den musikalske ål, copyright © 1960 by Benny Andersen
Den indre bowlerhat, copyright © 1964 by Benny Andersen
Kamera med køkkenadgang, copyright © 1965 by Benny Andersen
Portrætgalleri, copyright © 1966 by Benny Andersen
Den sidste øh, copyright © 1969 by Benny Andersen
Her i reservatet, copyright © 1971 by Benny Andersen
Personlige papirer, copyright © 1974 by Benny Andersen

The Lockert Library of Poetry in Translation is
supported by a bequest from the late Lacy Lockert, scholar
and translator of Corneille, Racine, and Dante.

Printed in the United States of America
by Princeton University Press, Princeton, New Jersey

This book is for Ellen and Ole Varming,
in appreciation of their friendship and help,
and at whose summer cottage in Liseleje
most of these translations were made.

PREFACE

These days when many of our poets exhibit a sameness in tone and subject matter from poem to poem, it is refreshing to encounter a writer with as many facets as Benny Andersen. His voice ranges from the somberness with which he invokes unearthly psychic distances in "Rural Station" to the rollicking humor of "Experiences," and his subjects from the mental anguish in "Autonomous" to the tender love of "Your Dress Without You" and "The Persistent Worshipper." In many of his nature poems, he not only creates a sharp, vivid picture, but by investing the scene with human correspondences, imbues the landscape with a marvelously whimsical perspective, as in "High and Dry":

> The spruce saws away at the horizon
> while the dunes cautiously
> peep out behind one another's shoulders.
> Low tide. The scowling black stones
> rise up and lick their lips
> with tongues of seaweed.
>
> Pale and bitter, the lighthouse stares
> at the gloating jaws of the boats—
> What distant shores have they tasted—
> What place could be more beautiful than this?
>
> A dried up starfish
> pointing in all directions.

Some of his other nature poems are less parabolic; instead of displaying whimsey, these poems evoke responses to the secretiveness of nature, as in the conclusion of "Relaxation":

> Bogsnails rise slowly to the surface.
> The mysteries of the deep
> have to come up and breathe.

Andersen's versatility extends to his use of language. He employs metaphors that surprise and startle us, as in the first line of "Certain Days": "The telephone's snakehead ready to strike." He uses metaphors as a vehicle for his energetic wit:

> Once in a garret in Esbjerg twenty years ago
> I was a popular resort for fleas
> functioned as a flea-hotel with meals included
> where the frisky delegations
> held successful gastronomical congresses.
>
> "Generation Gap"

Part of the excitement of Andersen's language lies in the fact that he is not restrained by a bookish concern with correctness. He uses new combinations of words, he makes up words, and he plays with grammar and syntax to achieve special poetic effects. In "Alcoholism" the staccato movement of the fragments conveys the feeling of a mind stunned by hangover:

> Dregsmorning.
> tapped for the last drop of impulse.
> shutters for the memory. nothing can intrude.
> shrivelheart. interestatrophy.

Andersen thinks his working-class background may have fostered his free use of language. Because people in the working class are not bound by genteel notions of correctness, they feel less constraint about innovating and experimenting, and they invent lively and sometimes irreverent metaphor. During one of our evenings together he recalled the time his uncle dropped in and commented on Benny's father: "Look at Svend, there; he's so thin we should give him a cherry soda and use him as a thermometer."

Andersen enjoys immense popularity in his native Denmark, but he is aware that his popularity may be based primarily on his humorous pieces rather than on the broad spectrum of his work. Believing that humor is interwoven with the tragic or sorrowful, he insists that he takes humor seriously, and rightly so—he can wield his complex, malleable humor as a scalpel, a club, or a caress. But humor for Andersen is also a way of making contact with his readers. After this contact, however, Andersen would like to deepen the relationship with his readers, to have his readers see that he is not only a humorist but an artist of many moods. Humor, then, serves as a means of drawing the reader in and exposing him to other landscapes of the mind. For this reason, Andersen's humorous poems are not segregated from his serious pieces. In fact, a grouping of poems such as the four prayers includes a wide range of moods and is a example of Andersen's technique in microcosm.

We see this characteristic ability of Andersen to present various tones and angles of vision not only in the totality of his work but within some individual poems as well. Consider the poem "Time." It begins in wordplay, with a comic exaggeration to point up the narrator's sense of the swift passage of time:

> We have twelve clocks in the house
> still it strikes me there's not enough time
> you go out to the kitchen
> get chocolate milk for your spindly son
> but when you get back
> he has grown too old for chocolate milk
> demands beer girls revolution

Yet the poem also expresses pensiveness and resignation in the lyrical line about the wife ("gently the widow awakes in her"), and then moves to a conclusion that is surreal, both witty and frightening at the same time:

You have to make the most of time in time
roam around a time without time and place
and when the time has come
call home and hear
"Are you calling 95 94 93 92?
That number is no longer in service."
Click.

Obviously an experience can be comic and sad, or absurd
and tender, simultaneously, but in reflecting upon an in-
cident, we have a tendency to sort out complex feelings
and to recall the experience as characterized by a single
feeling or tone. What is so striking about poems like
"Time" is that Andersen is able to fuse those feelings that
we tend to sort out. It is this fusion, this re-creation of a
totality of experience, that makes such poems so convincing
and powerful. In poems like "Time," Andersen is seriously
comic and comically serious.

Of course, not all of Andersen's poems are characterized
by such rich tonal ambiguity. He is also a master of friend-
ly satire, many of his poems exposing the follies and frailties
of human kind, but exposing them with a warmth and
generosity that seem to say: "Yes, I know, I too am im-
plicated":

I pray for those weak in spirit
(the crossword puzzle was hard today)

for those weak in flesh, for those hooked on the bottle
(I have an empty bottle for every stern intention)
"Skeptical Prayer"

One of the particular appeals of Andersen is his ability to
prick the pretensions of people, himself included. For ex-
ample, in "Analysis" the author pokes fun at the human
tendency to overindulge the imagination when confronting
reality, and then brings the narrator rudely to earth in the
comic incongruity of the last stanza:

A waterstain on the ceiling over the bed
resembles a rare orchid—
but what good is it on the ceiling?
First and foremost it resembles a waterstain.
. . .
Last night I found my philosophy,
and never have I slept so good.
But where will I find an excuse
for my having overslept?

Benny Andersen has become as well known in Denmark
as that other Andersen, Hans Christian; and it is possible
that the contemporary Andersen will become known and
admired by the world outside Denmark, as Hans Christian
was before him. Currently Benny Andersen is the most
popular poet in Denmark. It is a peculiar mark of the
separation of the artist and public in America that the adjective "popular" is pejorative, so one feels impelled to
add that Andersen has become a popular poet without sacrificing the integrity of his art.

ACKNOWLEDGMENTS

Thanks are due to the following magazines in which some of these translations first appeared: *Contemporary Literature in Translation, The Lines Review, Maine Edition, Modern Poetry in Translation, Prism-International, Trans-Pacific,* and *The West Coast Review.* I am also deeply indebted to Benny and Signe Andersen for their generous help with these translations, as well as to many other Danes who have generously given me advice, among them Poul Borum, Niels and Marianne Jensen, Niels Kofoed, Bjarne Kastberg, Eliza and Torben Kehlet, Else Mathiesen, Sven Nielsen, Ole and Ellen Varming, and many students at Jonstrup Seminarium. Sverre Arestad, Nadia Christensen, Herbert Goldstone, Edna Hong, Victor Kaplan, Carol Orr, James Scully, and Milton Stern gave me invaluable critical advice, for which I am deeply grateful. I wish to thank The American Council of Learned Societies and The American Philosophical Society for grants for the study of Danish Literature. These translations grew out of that study. Finally, I wish to thank the Connecticut Commission on the Arts for a grant which enabled me to prepare the manuscript for publication.

BIOGRAPHICAL NOTE

Benny Andersen was born in 1929 in Copenhagen. After graduating from secondary school, he went to work for an advertising agency while furthering his education in evening school. He had private musical training as a youth, and from 1949 to 1962 he earned his living by playing the piano in nightclubs and restaurants throughout Scandinavia. His continuing interest in music is reflected in the imagery and rhythms of his poetry. His first book of poems, *Den musikalske ål* ("The Musical Eel"), appeared in 1960 and won immediate public and critical acclaim. Other books of poetry followed: *Den indre bowlerhat* ("The Inner Bowler Hat") in 1964, *Kamera med køkkenadgang* ("Camera with Kitchen Privileges") in 1965, *Portrætgalleri* ("Portrait Gallery") in 1966, *Den sidste øh* ("The Last Er") in 1969, *Her i reservatet* ("Here on the Reserve") in 1971, and *Personlige papirer* ("Personal Papers") in 1974. His *Svantes viser* ("Svante's Songs"), published in 1973, is a novel which contains the poems of the main character, Svante. The poems are interspersed among the prose chapters, and Andersen's musical compositions for the songs are included in an appendix. Mr. Andersen has also published two collections of short stories and has written several children's books, as well as film scripts and television plays. His most recent book is a collection of essays and reminiscences, *Barnet der blev ældre og ældre* ("The Child Who Got Older and Older"). He has won numerous awards for his work, including The Louisiana Prize, The Workers Fellowship Cultural Prize, and The Critics Prize. He is married to the painter Signe Plesner Andersen, and they have two children.

A NOTE ON THE TRANSLATIONS

It is my hope that these translations catch something of the tone and style of the originals. I have attempted to be as literal as possible, although I have not hesitated to make changes where these changes moved the English versions closer to the spirit of the Danish texts. For example, wordplays in Danish that were impossible to reproduce in English were replaced by equivalent English wordplays either in the same line or somewhere else in the poem. I have also on occasion been less than literal in order to create equivalent sounds and rhythms in the English versions when I could do so without changing the essential meaning of the original lines. Mr. Andersen has generously devoted a great deal of time to reading and commenting on the English translations, often making valuable suggestions for the English versions. No changes in the literal meaning of the poems were made without his permission. There were some poems we both agreed should not be translated because too much would be lost in the process. I am aware, of course, that much is always lost in translation. I hope, however, that these translations can stand as poems in English and serve to introduce Benny Andersen's poetry to the English-speaking world.

Alexander Taylor

CONTENTS

PREFACE   vii
ACKNOWLEDGMENTS   xiii
BIOGRAPHICAL NOTE   xv
A NOTE ON THE TRANSLATIONS   xvii

from "The Musical Eel"

Rural Station   3
Analysis   5
The Forgotten Son   6
Morning Prayer   8
Winter Prayer   9
Table Prayer   10
Skeptical Prayer   11
Tenderness   12
Obituary   13
Headliner   14
Widescreen   15
Photographs   16
Sleepless Hours in the Summer House   17
The Musical Eel   18
The Critical Frog   19

from "The Inner Bowler Hat"

Goodness   20
Friendship   22
Slug-a-bed   24
Happiness   26
It's High Time   27
Smile   29
Memories   31

                                               xix

from "Camera With Kitchen Privileges"

Charity Concert 32
Relaxation 33
Jelly Fish 34
High and Dry 35
In the Bar 36
Autonomous 37
Optimist 38

from "Portrait Gallery"

This Is 39
Certain Days 41
M. 43
The Pampered Mermaid 44
The Hanged Informer 45
The Persistent Worshipper 46

from "The Last Er"

Experiences 47
Just to Be Sure 49
Dear Enemies 50
Dear Friends 51
Alcoholism 52
Generation Gap 53
Earthworm 54
This Uncertainty 55
Between Us 56
Your Dress Without You 57
The Last Er 60

from "Here on the Reserve"

All This 61
Love Declaration (woman to man) 62
Love Declaration (man to woman) 63
Now It's Said 64
Time 66

from "Personal Papers"

Life is Narrow and High   68
Sabina   69
Melancholy   71
A Hole in the Earth   72

BENNY ANDERSEN

SELECTED POEMS

Rural Station

One March day you're sitting
numb in a cold train.
With a hyperdermic needle
you are shot into the heart of Jutland.

The train suddenly halts,
tossing you out of yourself
here where dark and
light blood meet.

Muddied fields
with blots of snow
keep a despondent eye
on heaven's white doors

like small boys
who haven't eaten
all their porridge and are afraid
of their mother.

A constellation of wild geese
streaks across the heavens.
Is it my name that in their harsh,
mocking and distorted way they fling down?

Hesitating, as if to investigate
how much you still dare see,
a cow loose from her tether comes
toward you through the mud.
Silently gives birth to a calf in the snow.

You turn back, dizzy,
lose your way in this strange land.
Forget path and errand.
Notice only how the thick earth of Jutland
clutches your shiny shoes.

Analysis

Two voices through the wall awaken me,
one dark and tired,
one zealously explanatory.
Sounds, intonations, not words.

A waterstain on the ceiling over the bed
resembles a rare orchid—
but what good is it on the ceiling?
First and foremost it resembles a waterstain.

At the top of the window a little bit of blue.
But what does that say about the weather tomorrow?
Yesterday's weather I have to remember myself.
Who knows if it is raining in Rønne?

Last night I found my philosophy,
and never have I slept so good.
But where will I find an excuse
for my having overslept?

The Forgotten Son

Cocksure my brother sallied forth into the world,
sang himself away between arms and dice.
Gladly he accepted the world on its terms,
which for him was the whirling maelstrom.
It cast him up on various coasts.
Bit by bit, by different detours,
he was drawn back to the family farm.
Here it was he first put himself together—
what a meeting—he merged with his defeat,
which Father came out and kissed.
O Father, had you only waited one day, one hour!
But nothing but the fatted calf would do
to feast such a welcome defeat.

Have I myself chosen the small victories,
whose meat long ago has been chewed white and dry?
Have I myself rationed your love,
these small treacherous love-rations?
Harmless for others certainly
like throwing snowballs at a tree,
like boys spitting against the wind.

Thy will be done, my Father.
My bundle is tied, in it a fat white thigh,
a three days' love-ration.
Then I'll be lost
between mountains and springs.
Thus will I flee from the smoke of my offering
which was never beaten to earth
but stood up stiffly like a pillar of shame.

Years will pass, Father,
years without love,
years without fatted calves.

And then when I have saved
a pocketful of defeat,
when my clothes are smeared with grime,
then I will approach you
with fierce tired steps:
Then you will have to love me!

Morning Prayer

Vibrant morning,
separate the sour from the sweet,
the inside from outside,
let knives of light scrape away
my core of sour pride
so that I can fear
when fear's hour strikes,
so that I can hear
where I shall join in
when the great music starts.

Winter Prayer

Winter, make me quiet
so I can hear the pain
in the closed trees,
in the mute birds,
in the water that scratches
under the ice
with the thin fingernails of children.
Winter, make me quiet
so I can hear your pain.

Winter, make me alert
so I can recognize you.
This induction current
that crooks my hand
when I want to open it,
is that you?
Are you tied up some place
transmitting distress signals right through my nerves?
Winter, make me alert
so I can find you.

Table Prayer

Give me today
my bread to butter.
Soft and hard shall meet
in my hands
and the butter's sunshine overwhelm
the bread's darkness.
Let me touch what we live on,
brown bread, yellow butter,
love.

Skeptical Prayer

I pray for those weak in spirit
(the crossword puzzle was hard today)

for those weak in flesh, for those hooked on the bottle
(I have an empty bottle for every stern intention)

Peace on earth, repose for all those persecuted!
(I am behind in my taxes)

I pray for those hit by polio, those pollinated by the atom
for those toothless and those with polyps
(one never knows)

I pray for balance in life
like the shopkeeper with his thumb on the scales:
just let it *look* right!

Tenderness

Spare me your admonitions!
How should I unfold myself unseen
(ah! at last entirely alone)
when the tiny splinter
that's always left after you've gone
makes my whole body swell
to one big finger that throbs:
Let me be. . .

Obituary

The wind slides in from the sea.
The ice holds.
The wind chews at the flames of a lighter.
Can't get it down.

Then kicks the leaves from four snowdrops,
crawls into my white shirt on the line,
moves up to the place where the head should be
and dies.

Headliner

Sirens—skull fracture—old woman
who has nothing but money on her mind.
The kids scramble up
and catch the rolling coins under their heels,
grownups become like children again,
but the heirs shout by the deathbed:
Is it true, Aunt Gunhild,
there's not even a quarter left?
And Auntie smiles wanly: Just think, children,
my headache has completely disappeared.

Widescreen

I wander chilly and bloodforsaken
and snap at the sunset.
Widescreen! Hollywood! Technicolor!
And glare down at the flagstones
stamped with greasy leaves.

Then a chestnut cracks at my feet.
A bright brown eye opens.
Beholds heaven and earth
for the first time.

Photographs

She stops and pauses for breath at the landing.
All those stairs, all those years—
Stands with the cold key in her hand
and listens for thieves.

Nonsense—there are only photographs in there,
good-natured, prominent eyes.
No one looks like that anymore.

At last she glides through the slot
like a thin letter to herself.

Sleepless Hours in the Summer House

What about the children—soon too grown-up
to stay home alone. . .
and in the composing room—how
will the Balkan-affair turn out
with the all too clumsy captions
and every other line ending blind. . .

At last the dream's rotary press hums
and, impotent, he sees his own obituary
go to press
unreadable because of misprints.

The Musical Eel

Ashes flick off the sun.
Awesomely the eyes of the snail circle:
what distances!

The duck lands on the lake
noisy as a needle
dropped on a scratched record.

The eel leaves the lake forever.
Looks back several times furiously.

The Critical Frog

The duck arranges his reflection
neatly around himself for the evening.
At last the right sensitivity
to the reed-warbler's glowing tones.
People stand still and listen on the path,
enabling the mosquitos to hit home
while the water rat discreetly
removes the noisy ducklings.

Only a small young frog conceals his ecstasy
behind a belch.

Goodness

I've always tried to be good
it's very demanding
I'm a real hound for
     doing something for someone
hold coats
  doors
    seats
get someone a job
   or something
open up my arms
let someone have his cry on my shirt
but when I get my chance
I freeze completely
some kind of shyness maybe
I urge myself—do it
fling your arms wide
but it's difficult to sacrifice yourself
    when somebody's watching
so hard to be good
    for more than a few minutes
like holding your breath
however with daily practice
I have worked up to a whole hour
if nobody disturbs me
I sit all alone
with my watch in front of me
spreading my arms
    again and again

no trouble at all
I am actually best
when I'm all alone.

Friendship

I come and unload
kick open the door before you open
trudge on in over you
        with my burdens and sacks
get you propped up in a chair
brace you with pillows and assurances
hold on tight now
the first sack is dumped over your head
used anxieties, ashdistrusts
        gnawed affronts
    peelings and adversitydregs
you've got to help me, this can't go on
lift your head and say: hold out!
now the second sack, burned-out plans
remnants of journeys, split future
        and mouldy expectations
you still have your arms free
smiling offer your hand: take courage
stand your ground!
thanks for these words, it feels a little better now
ready for the third and last sack
with a little of everything, reversed visors
cans there have been wars in
grubby maps of sore points
the dead that walk again for a firm
let us remember Amanda in the peat bogs
our stiffly-whipped puberty
everything for you and only for you

I turn my pockets inside out
     the last I have
a little soulscratch a little greetingwool
     a single caramel
do you understand me now
     down under there
I knock the top off, dig breathingholes
down to your face, press my ear to the pile
hear you groan overwhelmed:
Stand firm and fight!
relieved I steal away
only a true friend talks like that.

Slug-a-bed

Immense impossible morning
where you never get out of bed
or even reach the edge of it
so far flung it is
large as a county
you worm your way
under the clammy lowhanging featherbed
lonesome lost spermatoza
in no condition to get there
have to stop
breathe air and courage
now no sweaty panic on the sheet
there are still untried creases to follow
no traffic to be careful of
you are expected out there at the featherbed-frontier
with questions, appointments, chutes, ties
you're expected to awaken
it's your duty to dig yourself out
once a day
and show up
eat a little
grow a little
stand in line waiting your turn
stretch
bow
sign something or dance
make up your mind
make your way
make do

but I'm all fagged out
because of all this featherbed
that pushes itself in front of me like a glacier
what is being transmitted through these feathers
send out a felt morse code
to toetapping authorities
tea rattling relatives
watchdog teachers and creditors
I am alive but enfeebled beforehand
start a search
with radar, frogmen, St. Bernards.

Happiness

There is something special about happiness
you can become wholly glad
when you meet it
but uneasy too
stand still a while
steal so gingerly forward
as if in a minefield
and every time you set your foot down
without being blown to pieces
you either forget to enjoy your happiness
or get sore over not knowing
how long it will last
so that when adversity finally turns up
it's a relief
as if you had reached safety
it's really a shame
because there is something special about happiness
which you otherwise don't meet
perhaps there's the fault
We know too little about it
We have to become better acquainted with it
I think it's a question of training.

It's High Time

It's high time
the water boils
the earth burns
the world is waiting
when Alexander was Caesar's age
he was already The Great
when Caesar was my age
he had had it
they did not waste time
time did not waste them
they used time like a shirt
slept with it on
ate with it on
were buried in it
and here I sit
hold newspaper
hold Christmas
hold back
let exploits walk by my nose
in hopeless arrears with experience
the world does not wait
when Mozart was five years
when Columbus weighed anchor
when Jesus was twelve
when Homer
when Rembrandt
when Pasteur
when Darwin
when Degas

when da Vinci
when da Gama
Damocles
Wencelaus
Wendt
it is high time
it is past time
my hat
my coat
my cycleclips
it is now or never

Smile

I was born with a howl
squalling I received my baptism
yelled when I was thrashed
shrieked when bees stung me
but gradually became more Danish
learned to smile at the world
at the photographer
    at doctors
        policemen and perverts
became a citizen in the land of the smile
smiles keep the flies away and the mind clean
and light and air are good for the teeth
if you arrive too late
if you go bankrupt
if you're run over
just smile
tourists stream in
to see smiling trafficvictims
the chuckling homeless
the cackling bereaved.

I can't get rid of my smile
sometimes I want to cry
or just stand openmouthed
or protest against other smiles
that conceal bloodthirstiness and putrefaction
but my own smile is in the way
sticks out like a cowcatcher
tearing hats and glasses off people
with a smile I bear my smile
        my halfmoon yoke
where one hangs his worries out to dry
I have to duck my head to the side
to get through a door
I am a citizen in the land of the smile
it's not a bit funny.

Memories

Sometimes memories of that time
                 whelm up in me
otherwise I am clearly better off now
that time
        I went to the dentist a lot
my fountain pen frequently blotted
once I thought
        my bicycle had been stolen
and I was very troubled about the future
which I now can see
        has gone very well
and yet my heart turns to jelly
        at the memories of that time
when I was never overwhelmed by memory.

Charity Concert

Black unemployed crow
hops around, his hands in his pockets,
at the bottom of the gravel pit.

Old dump car
thrums up, playing two rusty strings
by ear.

The crow flaps off, laughing scornfully.
But the dump car curtsies like a seasoned actor
at the brink of the pit.

Relaxation

The pond in the evening
dissolved time
twigs and insects
hands and numbers
finally move freely among each other.
Bogsnails rise slowly to the surface.
The mysteries of the deep
have to come up and breathe.

Jelly Fish

Rocking into a corner of the harbor
they learn to fathom security.
The current's blind encouragement
and exhausted backsplash.
In front of the last bar stinking of oil
the still pusating notes flock
da capo da capo.
Under the wharfs the sharp teeth of the mussels
and cunning engulfing seaweed.
But the prophesying onshore wind
youth's weather out there:
we live
we breathe
we journey
on many levels
on top
deserted parachutes
farther down luminous
huddled constellations.
In front of an endless bar
the softly splashing plea
da capo da capo.

High and Dry

The spruce saws away at the horizon
while the dunes cautiously
peep out behind one another's shoulders.
Low tide. The scowling black stones
rise up and lick their lips
with tongues of seaweed.

Pale and bitter, the lighthouse stares
at the gloating jaws of the boats—
What distant shores have they tasted—
What place could be more beautiful than this?

A dried up starfish
pointing in all directions.

In the Bar

Here gather small men with great voices
children of unwanted parents
around an overpopulated piano,
dreaming of handles, thick letters,
pregnant telephones
a life capped with foam.
Why live in a camera
with kitchen privileges
papered with null and void lottery stubs
cold showers for a hobby
and when sleep's plaster is ripped off
you find the day's abyss beneath you.
Here you do not leap from thumbtack to thumbtack
here the speeding seconds coagulate
here you shrug off your pain
and get it back again like minced melodies
the soft forcemeat of the heart.
Here it is possible to believe
that the frame causes the picture
that all is good if only
we put the right words in the mouth of the echo.
We spin safe grooves
on intoxication's tranquil spiral
until the street outside is only
a little scratch in our dream's LP-record.

Autonomous

I push a button
and the white lamp yellows and ripens.
I open the drawer where I keep
my consciousness
in small bundles in rubber bands.
I am master of this room.
My own feet under my own table.
I can put thumbtacks on one chair
and sit down safely on another.
On the windowsill
the plants take each other by the hand
and form a chain
to keep me from falling out the window.

But when I close my eyes
I see faces
      faces
        faces.

Optimist

I held you tightly
among black umbrellas.
They jammed us in,
stuck us in the eyes and cheeks.
We held the line in the archway
in the street of umbrellas.
But soon they got reinforcements.
Up from briefcases
Down the stairways
more black umbrellas kept on coming.
We turned between their cog-wheels.
Got inane tattoos,
ragged ears,
weaponless among the black umbrellas.
One day the sun will shine,
I said
in an egg of black umbrellas.
But then you shouted:
The sun is shining!
They attacked
and carried you off.
I was left alone
in the radiant sun.

This Is

This is the large city where we live
This is the narrow street in the large city where we live
This is the old house in the narrow street in the large city
                                                    where we live
This is you in the house
yes this is you
and this is me
in the middle of a sentence
in the middle of a TO that stretches in all directions
like a caterpillar at the end of a straw
This is the TO that turns about at the end of something
that isn't going any further at the moment
like a mast-acrobat I saw as a child
the mast was high and wobbled and swayed
eight meters to each side according to my father
I got a devil of a pain in my neck from looking so high
but got off really cheaply in comparison with the masterful
                                                    daredevil
who later
or was it his predecessor
broke mast and neck
This is the neck which bears the head which remembers the neck
which sooner or later fell down from the swaying mast
and broke against the pavement of the street in the suburb
where I stretched my neck toward the presumptuous
and from this stems my later weakness for climbing
shipmasts powerpoles eventually streetlights
This is the pupated person
who came from the child beside the mast in the suburb

to the large city where we live
the swinging capitol at the end of the road
which went through my clinging suburb
my neckaching childhood
my trialclimbing youth
This is the spine that leads up to the neck
which bears the head which uses the eyes
which saw the acrobat sway at the end of the mast
in the suburb that clings to the large overcrowded city where we
live
This is the head that sways at the top of the still erect spine
before your eyes
eight thoughts to each side
These are your eyes that are aimed at the TO
that I caught sight of at the end of the swaying mast
in the childhood I now have climbed up from
to the point where I can go no further
This is the TO
and this is you
yes this is you
Reach me a little finger.

Certain Days

The telephone's snakehead ready to strike
ominous crackling behind the wallpaper
certain days
when your clothes smell of shipwrecks and dungeons
even before you creep into them
you choke at the mere sight of your tie
days when it's smartest to crumble away under the covers
repent your past to get some peace of mind
let it blow over
sweat it out

Certain days
when the foot of the bed is a rendezvous for scorpions,
beaks of vultures and ice-cold cheeks of drowning friends
when you rush out and buy lottery tickets wholesale
and in keen competition with the Boy Scouts
herd old people across the street by the score
give directions with shaking fingers and simultaneously
nose about for fires be on the lookout for rooftiles
that can put an end to your life at any minute
sweat at the memory of all the vanished opportunities
to lend money and aid swans stuck in ice
put your own ears in order
put it off
make it good
even though you have milkcans of spilt milk in your past
the future can surely still count on you

just a respite
certain days that leave you
with just the skin on your nose and one and a half feet on the
ground
these days when you have to begin all over again every time

M.

Over my bed hangs a crucifix
for me love is holy
I look over my lover's shoulder
and meet the crucified one's sorrowful glance
but my lover notices
gets jealous
doesn't understand
stops
and I have to hang the son of man out in the kitchen
on a hook with the dishtowels
but I leave the door ajar
and when we lie in a certain way I can see
my saviour through the crack
he nods in at us: and this too I take upon me
And then when it really hurts
I get the most out of it
when it really hurts
I feel that the thorn-crowned
sees to it that it rightly comes to pass
that I suffer
the thorns thrust into my flesh
the veil is rent from top to bottom
I bear my share of the world's suffering
it is finished.

The Pampered Mermaid

Sweet they call me
but it's my salt they wish to lick
warmly they think of me
but it's my fishblood that eggs them on
the dreamers with drinking straws
the suitors with goldthreaded seines
drawn to me they say
because I am so standoffish
What are their soft fingers and bland glances
compared with the eightarmed back home
eight hundred suction cups know me inside and out
Every night I swim out
with a shoal of charmjellyfish following me
While I sink inkbefuddled
they are washed up onto the beach
  they wish it so
  I wish it so
In wordless agreement
they need salt
and I have to have air every now and then.

The Hanged Informer

Not everything in print is true
I didn't rat on him, on the contrary looked after him
when he came with bitter accusations because we were
                                        surrounded
That the others didn't endure
There's a rat in the woodpile somewhere they said
and they were the ones who wrote the story

Not in a tree as they claim
you stood there as a boy
when they carried me up out of the cellar
and have since wondered why
And all that about the thirty pieces of silver
who would rat on his best friend for thirty pieces of silver
I made good money as a bike repairman during the occupation
when cars were put up on blocks
No, I went into the corner where I used to hang up bikes that
                                        needed repair
and hanged myself because my best friend was killed
and the others were no longer my friends
but they were the ones who wrote the story.

The Persistent Worshipper

If just one single time I
could see you from within
send a homemade dragonkite up from your highest heartpeak
wave with gailycolored festoons and swallow-tailed flags from
                                        your eyebalconies
I who otherwise never give my blood away
herewith promise you a future on flying carpets made from our
                                        common membranes
to track down your mislaid lists of wishes
write all your Christmas cards a full ten years ahead
educate eventual children in all the disciplines
and keep your footsteps warm besides
If I am allowed to sail in your own sea
cross your gill reefs
be washed ashore on your most secret island
climb your spinal column's swaying palm
culminate as a cocoanut in your crown
I beg you at least answer my bottle-message
if I have objectionable failings just name them
and I will immediately have myself amputated to a toothpick if
                                        necessary
If only I might weed out intrusive grapeseeds and dreamshells
                                        from your teeth
get a single mother-of-pearl nail to clean as my reward
after that crack me
        cast me aside
I beg of you just
        Use me.

Experiences

Take it easy, says the weightlifter.
Just don't let yourself get knocked out, says the boxer.
It takes time to train a liontrainer, growls the lion.
Empathy, declares the dissipated rake.
Still water runs deepest,
sings the welldigger noisily.

Experience is a kind of evacuation
it's a relief to get over with
and exhibit for self-conscious glances:
see the great experience I have had
which isn't easy to ignore

"The reason that birds can fly is that
otherwise their wings will degenerate."
"Woman is man's superior in certain points
and vice versa."
"Art is dead."
"Art is politics."
"Everything is art."
"Life is a game."
"Life is death's hot dog."
"The seen depends on the eyes that see."
"The eye depends on the seen it sees."
"An apple a day keeps the doctor away
if you hit him right."

Now and again one gets the irresistible urge
to sit right down
and make his own shit.

Just to Be Sure

I am almost certain that my carpenter's rule
measures its own length when I open it out entirely
but just to be sure I have bought
another carpenter's rule of the same length
and until now they have measured the same
but what about the day when one of them measures wrong
how shall I know which one is right?
Just to be sure
I'll have to buy one more carpenter's rule.

Dear Enemies

I more than respect him
his successful goldbricking
has never gone to his head
so we cross paths without tripping each other up
hold out our hands before our feet
seek each other out beneath transparent friendshipmasks
carnival for two
give awards to each other's crafty disguises
celebrate old enmities
skoal diverging paths
pump each other for faux pas
and other rumornourishment
but observe strictly
that the balance of schemes is maintained
rumor for rumor scheme for scheme
and when we part as good enemies
wishing each other bad luck
have a shitty time
drive dangerously, etc.
it's just a manner of speaking on my part
for I would hate to lose my only enemy.

Dear Friends

I have two friends
who are enemies
and two enemies
who are friends.
One of my friends is friends with one of my enemies.
My other friend is an enemy of my other enemy's friend
It is difficult to keep straight
whom one should watch out not to say what to.
A reconciliation would simplify the situation considerably
so I really make a point of
turning the other cheek
but have at last run out of cheeks
try to mobilize my friends' cheeks.
That has made one of my enemies friendly
and one of my friends unfriendly.
My other enemy has become an enemy of his friend
and my other friend has become friends with my
other enemy's former friend
but also an enemy of his own former friend.
I vigorously contemplate forgetting the whole thing
pulling in my cheeks
and getting a fresh start.

Alcoholism

Dregsmorning.
tapped for the last drop of impulse.
shutters for the memory. nothing can intrude.
shrivelheart. interestatrophy.
vitamindistant. dreamedout. vaccinatedthrough
against fear. stripped of anxieties.
castrated from panic. only
the seismographic quivering of a hand. a
tremor somewhere. or once. faint
deflection at forgotten. or non-existing
center. circles spread out long after
the fish has jumped in the water. the fish
long since lies on the bank wiggling
with the hook in its mouth. the day's first
glass. and the next. and. not to assuage.
no longer in order to assuage. no more to assuage.
only. only to. only to quench.
to. only. out with it. thus.
only to quench an all consuming fatigue.

Generation Gap

Once in a garret in Esbjerg twenty years ago
I was a popular resort for fleas
functioned as a flea-hotel with meals included
where the frisky delegations
held successful gastronomical congresses.

They had more than enough in me
but I had more than enough of them
so one evening
I pumped my attic full of insect powder
shut the attic window and went to bed
damn near not waking up the next morning
half choked with DDT
The wretches vanished
and I myself was almost included in the bargain.

Think twenty years after
to be able to tell your children such a cock and bull story
They only know fleas in a flea circus
and stare at me half-doubting half-adoring
as if I had said:
By the way I got elephants once . . .

Earthworm

Earthnearest of all
most different from birds
sodsensitive sandticklish claylustful
you never enter any city's Coat of Arms
unfit for cantatas and ads
too unheroic
too naked
your indecent intercourse with the subsoil
wakes filthy thoughts in us
which can only lead us astray
but the worst is
that we are helplessly indebted to your obscene diligence
without you the globe would be sterile and fantasyforsaken
shame on you
all of the fertile green flowering surface
is your lecherous work
and for that we will never forget you
your low underdeveloped ludicrous
lower dishonorable blunted
lowest lowestcreeping sneaking proletarian
know your place and if you dare show yourself here on the surface
with righteous spades we stand ready
to amputate you from yourself.

This Uncertainty

When I at last perceived that it was certainly
not me you had said it about and it was certainly
not it you had said and it was certainly not you
who had said it I got nervous for real for what
can you now not find not to say the next time
you perhaps did not say something about me.

Between Us

Between your hands and your face
your blue blouse stirred by your heart
My eyes at most a meter from your smile
Between us sun and naked air
I'll soon promise you an appletree
or an art collection
Machinegunbursts from the firing range
only makes your blouse seem all the more authentic
In the fraction's-pauses between the shots
I can hear hair grow
We are simultaneous like two butterflywings
and it will be spring in ten minutes.

Your Dress Without You

Your clothes in a heap on the floor
hastily torn off
have been busy catching a bus
yet hardly take the bus naked
have certainly changed to slacks and jersey

A pair of tipped over shoes
pantyhose and underwear twisted together
and your dress without you
your plum colored bargain
bought with your own money
I know it well but I'm a little amazed
suddenly to see it lie there
collapsed—twisted—
as if struck by lightning

Had the times been other
the place and the situation
you might think there had been a battle
and chase mercenaries, Wends, Indians
but here and now it's most likely
that you have had to catch a bus

Your dress without you
I smooth out
to hang it up with the others
of different color length width
which have you in common
and which insignificantly tell me something
I remember well when we bought the material
for the Paisley-patterned one I remember
how you felt through the silk material
of the many colored one I remember
the first I bought for you myself
you know the green pleated dress that got longer
and longer with every wash and had to be cut off
and taken up every time for otherwise
you would gradually have had to walk on stilts
I remember remember but can not talk with you
as long as you aren't here
those wellhung rags without body or legs
and eyes
without answers
without you
this plumcolored which I will always remember
because it lies there unconscious without you.

I thrust my hand up under it
to rouse it up
twist my arm firmly in the sleeve
shake my hand in the twisted straitjacket
Punch and Judy as Blind Man's Buff
stare
get my other hand up through the neckline
it waves deprecatingly with its fingers
which I jerk back in fright from the scarecrow
so that it turns half inside-out
stare at your dress without you
stare at something that doesn't stare back
try to lay the dress down again
in the same disorder
difficult to reconstruct something carelessly dropped
difficult to pretend that it's nothing
difficult to ignore you
without you

The Last Er

Departure nine-thirty
not for ever
but anyhow
the train looks like
it could travel very far

"The time goes fast
once you are there . . ."
You try to say
a little more than er

Doorlids slam shut
buttonholes choke their buttons
hands are beginning to fall from sleeves
the train slowly tears itself loose
no one gets the last er
smiles sink backward into the mouth.

All This

Here in winter
you often catch yourself
thinking of summer
the glum boat by the beach
wet people
folding gulls
popsicles beers and bonfires
uncold cheeks and mittenfree togetherness
the heart lies right under the sun
it wouldn't surprise you to see
a horse rise out of the deep with dreaming eyes
the day is full of melancholy muscles
you lie in the stonefree sand
with another's hand in your own
the heart right under the sun
the sun right under the heart
waves lapping in one ear
and out the other
back and forth
a gentle form of brainwashing
until you feel and know
that all this and heaven too
    will one day be taken from us.

Love Declaration
(woman to man)

Take off your hat, my friend
and your handsome wellingtons
your nose is cold
but your mouth is warm
when I take an impression of your expected eyes
your voice so welcome-beautiful
I get the urge to roll great red carpets
                              out of both ears
and your delicate cough gives me pangs
manchild, boyfather
person with a cough
button-expert friend
my welcoming speech has begun
you are the opposite of a splinter
a splinter in the finger
hurts in a single little spot
but you do good all over
                    all under
and long after in all directions
luke-warm friendships blaze up
tired aunts smile uncontrollably
the neighbor's children ask for good advice
and I myself can more than live with myself
you do such good
so: do it!

Love Declaration
(man to woman)

Here yes
you my rendezvous my clearness yes
my "your"
our different oneness
to analyze you more exactly yes
in breasts philosophies thighs origins eyecolor
but you are indivisible
to be your nearest surroundings makes me bigger
than anything that anyone has hoped for me
god and child and life's clown
it is almost too much
therefore beneficent with your small defects
you darling with breasts and fellow beings
I love you
who make me love more than you
we are caught in this century
which holds so many containers
which can contain the incredible
but all too seldom do it
I am your proud neighbor
(I who have detested pride)
impossible to give it up
with you as one's nearness.

Now It's Said
(Man, about 30)

If a paving stone came flying at me
I think I would duck
so it struck another
yet not maintain because of that
that the best defense is self-defense
I am least of all out for myself
often cannot really find myself
so when I really have to get myself together
I have to call myself into session

I have perhaps a little too much to do
with bending question marks into exclamation points
too often take off my head for the secure
who make the world insecure for the insecure
perhaps admire indignation's athletes
who can take offense up to ten times a day without tiring
am too busy to support supporters
whom I otherwise would have had for support

I well know that I don't always do the right thing
but on the other hand find it easy to do that
    which is a little different from the wrong
so don't stamp me as silent and passive
don't confuse me with sardines

I don't yet come in cans
who dares judge
how far my ears are out
and how long afterward I think over what I've heard
a night
a year
no one knows
no one shall boast about
being able to serve my silence up on a slice of bread
in oil or tomato sauce
and get from me a taste of the majority
don't misuse my silence
for then I'll begin to stammer
don't wake the sleeping lion in me
it already sleeps poorly

Even if I contribute abundantly
to law and order and (not least) peace
I am no stranger to conviction
I am not blind to the aim of stonethrowing
and if there's one thing I'm not without
it's humor
so I can say with a smile
if paving stones are thrown
and barricades built from them
then just pave all the streets with asphalt.

Time

We have twelve clocks in the house
still it strikes me there's not enough time
You go out to the kitchen
get chocolate milk for your spindly son
but when you get back
he has grown too old for chocolate milk
demands beer girls revolution
You have to make the most of your time while you have it
Your daughter comes home from school
goes out to play hopscotch
comes in a little later
and asks if you'll mind the baby
while she and her husband go to the theater
and while they're in the theater
the child with some difficulty
is promoted to 10th grade
You have to make the most of your time while you have it
You photograph your hitherto young wife
with fullblooded gypsyheadscarf
an opulent fountain in the background
but the picture is hardly developed
before she announces that it is nearly
her turn to collect social security
gently the widow awakes in her
You would like to make the most of your time
but all the time it stays away
what becomes of it
was it ever there at all

have you used too much time
in drawing time out
You have to make the most of time in time
roam around a time without time and place
and when the time has come
call home and hear
"Are you calling 95 94 93 92?
That number is no longer in service."
Click.

Life is Narrow and High

A matchstick flares in space
briefly lights up a face before it dies.
In the dark hands meet
briefly touch before they stiffen.
Words are sent out.
Some few get to reach an ear
are perhaps remembered a while.
Measured lengthwise life is short
but measured vertically infinite
a quivering fiber in death's muscle.
Kiss right now
before your kiss strikes a skull.
Soon you will be no one
but now you have lips
and matches.

Sabina

I do not know you, Sabina,
I do not know anyone having that name
but I think you're wonderful and warm like your name
and dangerous for those of my sex.
I have never met you, Sabina,
and it's certainly just as well,
for then I would have become so hectic
I'd have forgotten everything else but you,
and then your lover—probably a Greek
Marxist—would have gunned me down,
And I love to live, Sabina, especially
after I have not met you.
You've changed my life considerably,
I've lost a good bit of weight
just to please you, Sabina.
I'm scarcely as good company as before,
but have become more conscientious.
On voting day I stand for a long while thinking:
Where would Sabina mark her ballot?
That's where I'll mark it, too,
for Sabina must certainly be supported.
Sabina, my secret angel,
you guide my hand and my thought,
and things are going quite smoothly, after all,
and when I die one day, Sabina,
hopefully I will hear
your warm voice proclaim:

"He could have been a lot worse.
He left his mark here and there,
he talked often with his children,
a few of his neighbors will miss him.
Perhaps he was a little confused
but it stemmed from an honest heart
and no one asked him for beer in vain
He was on time for his meals
and slandered himself most of all.
There weren't many of his kind
and he should be thanked for that."
Then I'll pass away peacefully
although it will certainly be
a curious sensation.
Thank you, Sabina, my guardian spirit—
I do not know you, Sabina,
I do not know anyone like you.

Melancholy

A teaspoon lies on the road
smashed flat by a cement truck.
A window is open
but nobody looks out.
Perhaps that's why no one
puts up a ladder and elopes with
the one who isn't looking out—
or has it already happened?
It's as if everyone has gone.
In a fit of ladderlessness
I pick up the teaspoon.
Oh, how flat it's become.
I'll never come here again.

A Hole in the Earth

A hole has come in the earth. Empty.
Without earth around it
it wouldn't be there at all.
The hole is deeply dependent on the earth,
an emptiness that shows something exists
something that shows this emptiness exists.
If the earth wasn't there
there would be no emptiness either.
From hole you have come
to earth you shall return.
Or vice versa.
I warmly pat the hole
and keep going on earth.

THE LOCKERT LIBRARY OF
POETRY IN TRANSLATION

George Seferis: Collected Poems (1924-1955), translated,
   edited, and introduced by Edmund Keeley and Philip
   Sherrard
Collected Poems of Lucio Piccolo, translated and edited by
   Brian Swann and Ruth Feldman
The Complete Poems of C. P. Cavafy, translated by Edmund
   Keeley and Philip Sherrard and edited by George
   Savidis
Selected Poems of Andrea Zanzotto, translated and edited by
   Ruth Feldman and Brian Swann
The Poetry of René Char, translated by Mary Ann Caws
   and Jonathan Griffin
The Poetry of Tudor Arghezi, translated and edited by
   Michael Impey and Brian Swann